WILD FLOWERS
OF DUNGENESS

A PHOTOGRAPHIC GUIDE

Barbara Gray & Heather Silk

Published May 2007
Reprinted November 2012

Printed by Judges of Hastings (01424) 420919
www.judges.co.uk

i

Contents

PREFACE

Barbara and I are both volunteers at the RSPB Dungeness Visitor Centre and have often been asked if there is a book about the many wild flowers of the area. We have been unable to find any flower books relating specifically to Dungeness, although both RSPB and Dungeness Bird Observatory do have species lists. Over the years, Barbara has taken many photographs of the flowers at Dungeness. We decided to use these to produce an introductory guide for which I would do the research and write the text. We have not done this for our own personal gain because we want to encourage other people to appreciate the wonderful flowers to be found in this unique habitat. Therefore all royalties (after printing costs) will be donated to wild plant conservation in the UK.

INTRODUCTION

Geology
The Dungeness peninsula in the south–east corner of Kent, is the largest shingle formation of its type in Europe and is a very rare habitat. There are similar areas in Japan and New Zealand. It occupies an area of approximately 12 square miles. This shingle has accumulated because of longshore drift moving pebbles (mostly flint) up the Channel in a west-east direction. Wave action during major storms has created hundreds of shingle ridges; the building up of these took over 5000 years. These ridges with many small stones are known as fulls and the valleys in between with larger pebbles are known as lows. There is more vegetation in the fulls than the lows because the smaller fine stones retain more water and allow seeds and humus to collect close to the surface in the spaces between them. The lows are almost void of vegetation.

Species variety and adaptations
Over 600 plant species are found at Dungeness, which is roughly a third of the whole number in the UK. Many are specially adapted to this specialised habitat. For example Sea Kale has very long roots to anchor it in the shingle and to reach moisture. Sea Campion has a waxy coating on the leaves to help prevent the water loss caused by growing in an exposed area and its creeping stems form cushions to keep it close to the ground to prevent wind damage. The hairs on Nottingham Catchfly help to conserve moisture. A high proportion of species belong to the Pea family, (mentioned as having pea shaped flowers in the text). This is because they can fix nitrogen in the air by means of bacteria in their root nodules, thus enabling them to live in poor soil.

Some plants manage to colonise by their seeds germinating in the build up of humus created when species such as Broom or Blackthorn die back. The lowering of the water table has meant the loss of some species but others have arrived to take their place. However some of these are garden escapes.

Conservation of Dungeness
The importance of Dungeness for its geology, uncommon insects, its unique botanical community and the variety of birds breeding and passing through, has led to its designation as a National Nature Reserve. Different organisations are involved in looking after the NNR. The Royal Society for the Protection of Birds own or lease 990 hectares, Natural England and the Romney Marsh Countryside Project manage the Point and Dungeness Bird Observatory is responsible for ringing birds, recording, monitoring and research.

Species location and further information
This book can only try to do justice to a limited number of species in this unique habitat and is meant as an introduction to the flora of Dungeness. It covers some of the commoner species and the shingle specialists plus some of the more unusual. Most of these may be easily seen from the Dungeness RSPB Nature Trail and all are within the National Nature Reserve. Each page has a box to tick the species found and the date may be added if so desired. If a flower is found that does not quite match the photograph or description, this may be a closely related species which is not included. A list of more detailed identification guides to consult may be found on page vi plus contact details for helpful organisations. Many of these have programmes of guided plant walks and flower identification days.

There is a glossary to help with botanical terms which we have tried to keep to a minimum.

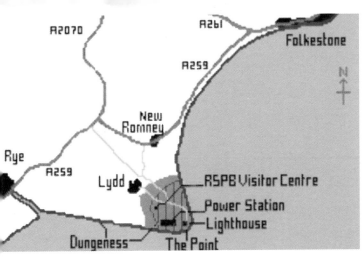

A2070   A261
                    Folkestone
         A259

New
Romney

Rye

A259
    Lydd   RSPB Visitor Centre
                  Power Station
                  Lighthouse
Dungeness   The Point

Blue hatching is the area covered by this book

Green is the NNR
Map not to scale

Shingle ridges from the top of the lighthouse

References and Further Reading

Wild Flowers of Britain and Ireland, by Marjorie Blamey, Richard Fitter and Alastair Fitter (A & C Black,2003).

Wild Flowers of Britain and Northern Europe, by Richard Fitter, Alastair Fitter and Marjorie Blamey (William Collins, 3rd edition 1978 and HarperCollins, 5th edition 1996).

Cassell's Wild Flowers of Britain and Northern Europe, by Marjorie Blamey and Christopher Grey-Wilson (Cassell, 2003).

The Wild Flower Key, by Francis Rose (Frederick Warne ,1991 and revised edition Frederick Warne, 2006).

Field Guide to the Wild Flowers of Britain, by Reader's Digest Association Ltd (Readers Digest Association Ltd, 1988)

Organisations for further information

Bumblebee Conservation Trust, School of Biological and Environmental Sciences, University of Stirling, Stirling. FK9 4LA. Tel:01786 467818.   Website:www.bumblebeeconservation.org.uk

Dungeness Bird Observatory, David Walker, 11,RNSSS Cottages, Dungeness, Romney Marsh, Kent. TN29 9NA. Tel:01797 321309. Website: www.dungenessbirdobs.org.uk

Kent Wildlife Trust, Tyland Barn, Sandling, Maidstone, Kent. ME14 3BD. Tel:01622 662012. Website: www.kentwildlife.org.uk

Plantlife International, 14 Rollestone Street, Salisbury, Wiltshire.SP1 1DX. Tel:01722 342 730. Website: www.plantlife.org.uk

Romney Marsh Countryside Project, Romney Marsh Day Centre, Rolfe Lane, New Romney, Kent. TN28 8JR. Tel:01797 367934. Website:www.rmcp.co.uk

Royal Society for Protection of Birds, Boulderwall Farm, Dungeness Road, Lydd, Kent. TN29 9PN. Tel:01797 320588. Website: www.rspb.org.uk/dungeness

The Wild Flower Society, 82A High Street, Sawston,Cambridge.CB2 4HJ. Tel:01223 830665. Website:www. thewildflowersociety.org.uk

GLOSSARY

Acid soil. Lacking lime but often rich in decaying organic matter.

Bract. Like a small leaf immediately below the flowers.

Calyx. All the sepals – these form a ring immediately below the petals and are usually green or brown.

Disc floret

Disc floret. A small flower, shaped like a tube, found in the flowerhead of members of the Daisy family. See picture.

Floret. A small flower, part of a flowerhead.

Leaflet

Flowerhead. Lots of very small flowers clustered together in a tightly packed head e.g. Daisies,Dandelions,Thistles and some others.

Gland. A tiny globe shaped tip to a leaf (or other part of plant), shiny and usually sticky.

Lip

Lanceolate. A spear shaped leaf with a point.

Leaflet. Part of a leaf. See picture.

Linear. A narrow leaf, almost parallel sided.

Lip. Lower (and sometimes upper part of a flower) where the petals are different shapes and sizes. See picture.

Pinnate leaf

Lobed. Dividing, but not separating completely.

Oblong leaf. About twice or three times as long as broad.

Oval leaf. More or less egg shaped, about twice as long as broad.

Parasitic. A plant, usually without green colouring, taking all its food from another plant to which it is attached.

Pinnately lobed

Pinnate leaf. A leaf with many opposite pairs of leaflets along the leaf stalk. See picture.

Pinnately lobed. A leaf with many opposite pairs of leaflets along the leaf stalk, however these are joined at the base. See picture.

Ray floret

Ray floret. A small flower, shaped like a strap, in or around the flowerhead of many members of the Daisy family. See picture.

Rosette. Flattened group of leaves at base of stem in a roundish rose shape.

Runner. Horizontal stem running above ground

Sepals. Form a ring immediately below petals, usually green or brown.

Shrub. Very branched woody plant, shorter than a tree.

GLOSSARY

Spike. Arrangement of flowers up a central stem like a cylinder. See picture.

Spike

Spur. A tube or pouch shaped projection, usually containing nectar and thin, coming from the back or base of a petal. See picture.

Spur

Stamen. Male part of the flower, found outside the centre of the flower, usually in a ring, consisting of a tip(anther) on top of a "stalk"(filament). See picture.

Stamen

Stigma. Female part of the flower which receives the pollen, found in the centre of the flower on top of a " column" (the style). See picture.

Tap root. Main root of a plant.

Stigma

Tendril. Grows usually from the end of a leaf, often coiled and twisted, sometimes branched.

Thorn. Sharp woody "spine", straight or curved.

Trefoil. A leaf divided into 3 leaflets. See picture.

Trefoil

Vein. A thickened line visible in a leaf (like the veins in the human body).

Whorl. A cluster of 3 or more leaves arising from the same point on a stem. See picture.

Whorl

REDSHANK *(Persicaria maculosa)* ☐

Height: Medium. **Flowers:** Pink or whitish, each flower 0.4 cm across, flowers crowded towards top of spike. **Stem:** Erect or sprawling, branched, reddish, swollen above point where leaf joins stem. **Leaves:** Lanceolate, often with black blotches. **Habitat:** Bare ground, waste places, often near water. **Flowering Time:** June–October. **Abundance:** Infrequent. **Extra info:** Also known as Redleg.

SHEEP'S SORREL *(Rumex acetosella)* ☐

Height: Low, short. **Flowers:** Reddish, very small, each flower 0.2 cm across. **Stem:** Erect or lying on the ground and rising at the end. **Leaves:** Shaped like a medieval pike–head. **Habitat:** Shingle, heaths, dry acid grassland. **Flowering Time:** May–August. **Abundance:** Very common. **Extra info:** Food plant for caterpillars of Small Copper butterfly.

RED CAMPION *(Silene dioica)* ☐

Height: Medium, tall. **Flowers:** Bright or pale pink, 5 forked petals, each flower 1.8–2.5 cm across. **Stem:** Erect, hairy. **Leaves:** Oval, pointed, hairy. **Habitat:** Hedgebanks, woodland. **Flowering Time:** March–November. **Abundance:** Occasional.

RAGGED ROBIN *(Lychnis flos–cuculi)* ☐

Height: Medium, tall. **Flowers:** Rose red, 5 deeply forked petals giving a ragged look, each petal split into 4, each flower 3–4 cm across. **Stem:** Erect, branching. **Leaves:** Lanceolate, rough. **Habitat:** Damp meadows, marshy areas. **Flowering Time:** May–August. **Abundance:** Occasional.

SOAPWORT *(Saponaria officinalis)* ☐

Height: Medium, tall. **Flowers:** Very pale pink or white, 5 petals, each flower 2.5 cm approx across, may be double flowered. **Stem:** Erect, branched. **Leaves:** Acute, 3–5 prominent veins. **Habitat:** Verges, hedges. **Flowering Time:** June–September. **Abundance:** Local, by entrance to RSPB Reserve. **Extra info:** Frequent garden escape, used at one time for washing wool and cloth.

DOG ROSE *(Rosa canina)* ☐

Height: 1–3 metres. **Flowers:** Pink or white, 5 petals, each flower 4–5 cm across. **Stem:** Arching, many hooked thorns. **Leaves:** 2–3 pairs of toothed oval leaflets. **Habitat:** Hedges, scrub. **Flowering Time:** June–July. **Abundance:** Occasional. **Extra info:** The fruit, rose-hips, was used to make syrup rich in Vitamin C.

COMMON POPPY *(Papaver rhoeas)*

Height: Medium. **Flowers:** Deep scarlet, 4 petals, often with a dark centre, each flower 7–10 cm across. **Stem:** Erect, with bristly hairs, usually branched. **Leaves:** Narrow toothed divisions, hairy. **Habitat:** Shingle, bare and waste places, arable fields, roadsides, disturbed ground. **Flowering time:** June–October. **Abundance:** Common.

BRAMBLE *(Rubus fruticosus)* □

Height: 1–3 metres. **Flowers:** Pink or white, 5 petals, often crinkly, each flower 2–3 cm across. **Stem:** Scrambling, arched, thorny. **Leaves:** Prickly, 3–5 oval toothed leaflets. **Habitat:** Hedges, scrub, waste ground. **Flowering Time:** May–November. **Abundance:** Very common. **Extra info:** Many recorded varieties.

<u>**SEA PEA**</u> *(Lathyrus japonicus)* ☐

Height: Low. **Flowers:** Purple, fading to blue, pea shaped, each flower 1.4–2.2 cm across, 5–15 flowers on a stem. **Stem:** Prostrate, angled. **Leaves:** Greyish green, 2–5 pairs of leaflets, oval, blunt, rather fleshy, sometimes without tendrils. **Habitat:** Shingle and dunes by sea. **Flowering Time:** June–August. **Abundance:** Rare.

<u>**GRASS VETCHLING**</u> *(Lathyrus nissolia)* ☐

Height: Short, medium. **Flowers:** Bright crimson red, each flower 1.0 cm across approx., pea–shaped, 1 or 2 together. **Stem:** Erect. **Leaves:** Narrow, like grass, hard to find! **Habitat:** Grassland. **Flowering Time:** May–July. **Abundance:** Infrequent.

REST – HARROW *(Ononis repens)* ☐

Height: Short, medium. **Flowers:** Pink. Each flower 1.0–1.5 cm long, pea–shaped. **Stem:** Creeping or ascending, hairy all round. **Leaves:** Blunt toothed, oval, sticky, hairy, with a harsh smell. **Habitat:** Dry grassy places, scrub, dunes. **Flowering Time:** June–September. **Abundance:** Fairly common.

RED CLOVER *(Trifolium pratense)* ☐

Height: Short, medium. **Flowers:** Pink–purple, flowerhead round or egg shaped 2–3 cm across, consisting of many small separate pea shaped flowers in a dense head. **Stem:** Hairy, usually erect. **Leaves:** In leaflets of 3, often with whitish crescent in centre, may be slightly pointed at tip. **Habitat:** Grassy places. **Flowering Time:** May–September. **Abundance:** Very common. **Extra info:** Bumble bees are very important for pollination.

HARESFOOT CLOVER *(Trifolium arvense)* ☐

Height: Low, short. **Flowers:** Pale pink or whitish egg–shaped flowerhead up to 2.5 cm long consisting of many tiny pea–shaped flowers. Flowerhead feels soft to the touch with lots of white hairs. **Stem:** Erect, branched. **Leaves:** Narrow leaflets in 3s, hairy on both sides. **Habitat:** Sandy grassland, dunes. **Flowering Time:** June–September. **Abundance:** Fairly common.

COMMON STORKSBILL *(Erodium cicutarium)* ☐

Height: Low, medium. **Flowers:** Purplish pink or white, 5 petals each 0.6–0.8 cm long, often unequal size, may have a black spot at the base. **Stem:** Erect, sometimes spreading, hairy, sticky. **Leaves:** Pinnate, divided. **Habitat:** Bare,grassy places. **Flowering Time:** April–September. **Abundance:** Common. **Extra info:** Seed head shaped like a bird's bill, hence the name. **Sea Storksbill** *(Erodium maritimum)* (not shown) also at Dungeness, has rapidly falling flowers up to 0.3 cm across and oval, toothed leaves in a rosette.

HERB ROBERT *(Geranium robertianum)* ☐

Height: Medium. **Flowers:** Pink, 5 notched petals, each flower 2.0 cm across. **Stem:** Erect, branched, hairy, often reddish. **Leaves:** Toothed, shaped like palm of a hand, few hairs. **Habitat:** Hedgebanks, rocks, shingle. **Flowering Time:** April–November. **Abundance:** Occasional. **Extra info:** Strong smelling.

CUT– LEAVED CRANESBILL *(Geranium dissectum)* ☐

Height: Short, medium. **Flowers:** Pink–purple, 5 petals, notched, flowerhead 0.8 cm across. **Stem:** Erect, branched, straggly. **Leaves:** Deeply divided, hairy. **Habitat:** Grassland, wasteland, hedgebank. **Flowering Time:** May–September. **Abundance:** Fairly common.

MUSK MALLOW *(Malva moschata)* ☐

Height: Medium, tall. **Flowers:** Rose pink or white, 5 separated notched petals, each flower 3–6 cm across. **Stem:** Erect, hairy. **Leaves:** Stem leaves deeply and narrowly cut. **Habitat:** Grassy areas, hedgebanks. **Flowering Time:** July–August. **Abundance:** Uncommon.

RED HEMP NETTLE (*Galeopsis angustifolia*) ☐

Height: Short, medium. **Flowers:** Deep rosy pink, white spots on lip, each flower 1.5–2.5 cm long, helmet shaped with a 3 lobed lower lip. **Stem:** Erect, branched, hairy. **Leaves:** Narrow, broader lower down stem, toothed edges. **Habitat:** Shingle beaches, bare stony areas, scarce in cornfields. **Flowering Time:** July–September. **Abundance:** Rare.

11

FOXGLOVE *(Digitalis purpurea)*

Height: Tall. **Flowers:** Pink purple, pale pink or white, bell shaped, 4–5 cm long, spotted inside, up to 80 all hanging on the same side of the stem. **Stem:** Erect, unbranched, downy. **Leaves:** Oval, lanceolate, wrinkled, downy. **Habitat:** Scrub, wasteland, woods, dry soil. **Flowering Time:** June–August. **Abundance:** Very common. **Extra info:** Was used as a heart medicine.

ROSEBAY WILLOW HERB *(Chamerion angustifolium)*

Height: Tall. **Flowers:** Bright pink–purple, 4 petals, slightly unequal, each flower 2–3 cm across. **Stem:** Erect. **Leaves:** Narrow, often with wavy edges. **Habitat:** Waste ground, open woods, heathland. **Flowering Time:** July–September. **Abundance:** Common. **Extra info:** Also known as Fireweed because often grows on ground cleared by fire.

GREAT WILLOWHERB *(Epilobium hirsutum)* ☐

Height: Tall. **Flowers:** Purplish–pink, 4 notched petals, each flower 1.5–2.5 cm across, prominent 4 lobed white stigma in the centre. **Stem:** Erect, branched, downy. **Leaves:** Narrow, downy. **Habitat:** Damp places. **Flowering Time:** July–August. **Abundance:** Common.

COMMON MALLOW *(Malva sylvestris)* ☐

Height: Medium, tall. **Flowers:** Rose purple, 5 separate notched petals with darker veins, each flower 2.5–4 cm across. **Stem:** Usually erect, may sprawl. **Leaves:** Shaped like palm of hand, often with small dark spot at base of leaf. **Habitat:** Roadside, waste land. **Flowering Time:** June–October. **Abundance:** Occasional.

SCARLET PIMPERNEL *(Anagallis arvensis)*

Height: Low. **Flowers:** Scarlet (rarely blue or pink), 5 blunt petals, star–like, each flower 1–1.5 cm across. **Stem:** Square, prostrate, creeping. **Leaves:** Pointed oval, black dotted beneath. **Habitat:** Cultivated areas, dunes. **Flowering Time:** May–October. **Abundance:** Common. **Extra info:** Also known as Poor Man's Weatherglass because flowers open in sunshine.

THRIFT *(Armeria maritima)*

Height: Low, short. **Flowers:** Dark to pale pink, 5 petals, each flower 0.8 cm across, many clustered together to form rounded flowerhead 1.5–2.5 cm across. **Stem:** Erect, brown sheath below flowerhead at top of stem. **Leaves:** Form a cushion, one veined, very narrow, like grass. **Habitat:** Cliffs, rocks, saltmarsh, coastal pastures. **Flowering Time:** April–October. **Abundance:** Fairly common. **Extra info**: Featured on the reverse of the old threepence piece, before decimalisation.

COMMON CENTAURY *(Centaurium erythraea)* ☐

Height: Low, short.
Flowers: Pink, 5 petals, each flower 1.0–1.2 cm across, flowers in groups branching from main stem.
Stem: Erect, branched.
Leaves: Narrow, oval, 3–7 prominent veins on each leaf. **Habitat:** Grassy places, dunes, woodland clearings. **Flowering Time:** June–September.
Abundance: Common.

SEA BINDWEED *(Calystegia soldanella)* ☐

Height: Low. **Flowers:** Pink with white stripes, trumpet shaped, each flower 2.5–4.0 cm across. **Stem:** Creeping. **Leaves:** Kidney shaped, fleshy. **Habitat:** Sand dunes, coastal. **Flowering Time:** June–September. **Abundance:** Occasional.

COMMON DODDER *(Cuscuta epithymum)* ☐

Height: Low. **Flowers:** Pale pink, appear to be 5 pointed petals, each flower 0.3–0. 4 cm across, bell shaped, scented, heads in tight rounded clusters. **Stem:** Climbing, scrambling red or orange thread–like tangle. Parasitic climber on Wood Sage (pg 60) Heather etc. **Leaves:** None. **Habitat:** Grassy places, shingle, heathland. **Flowering Time:** June–October. **Abundance:** Very common. **Extra info:** Also known as Devil's Guts, from its climbing habit.

RED VALERIAN *(Centranthus ruber)* ☐

Height: Medium, tall. **Flowers:** Red, pink or white, 5 joined petals, fragrant, each flower 0.5 cm across. **Stem:** Erect, branched. **Leaves:** Pointed oval or lanceolate, greyish green. **Habitat:** Shingle, walls, steep banks, cliffs, rocks, quarries. **Flowering Time:** May–September. **Abundance:** Common.

SLENDER THISTLE *(Carduus tenuiflorus)* ☐

Height: Short, medium, tall. **Flowers:** Pale pink, flowerheads 0.8 cm across, in dense cylindrical brush like clusters, bracts below flowerheads with outward curved spines. **Stem:** Erect, narrowly branched, spiny, greyish cottony. **Leaves:** Spiny, pinnately lobed, spiny tipped, cottony white underneath. **Habitat:** Grassland, roadside, hedgebanks, wasteland, often by sea. **Flowering Time:** May–August. **Abundance:** Very common.

COMMON KNAPWEED *(Centaurea nigra)* ☐

Height: Short, medium. **Flowers:** Red–purple or pink, flowerhead 2–4 cm across, like a brush, black bracts beneath flowerhead. **Stem:** Erect, rough, grooved, hairy. **Leaves:** Narrow, thin. **Habitat:** Grassy places, roadsides. **Flowering Time:** June–September. **Abundance:** Uncommon.

***

Alternative Colours: Nottingham Catchfly is included in the white section, but may also be pink.

CUCKOO FLOWER *(Cardamine pratensis)*

Height: Medium. **Flowers:** Lilac or white, 4 petals, each flower 1.2–2.8 cm across. **Stem:** Erect. **Leaves:** Upper leaflets narrow with few hairs. **Habitat:** Damp places, moist woodland, by streams. **Flowering Time:** April–June. **Abundance:** Infrequent. **Extra info:** Caterpillars of the Orange Tip butterfly feed on the developing seed pods.

TUFTED VETCH *(Vicia cracca)*

Height: Tall. **Flowers:** Purplish blue violet, pea shaped, each flower 1.0–1.2 cm long, 10–40 all on one side of a spike. **Stem:** Clambering, slightly downy. **Leaves:** Pairs of 8–12 narrow leaflets, curly tendrils at the end. **Habitat:** Hedges, bushy places, scrub. **Flowering Time:** June–August. **Abundance:** Common.

BUSH VETCH (*Vicia sepium*) ☐

Height: Medium, tall. **Flowers:** Blue violet, pea shaped, each flower 1.2–1.5 cm long, 2–6 flowers together in a short spike. **Stem:** Clambering, downy. **Leaves:** Pairs of 3–9 oval leaflets, with curly tendrils at the ends. **Habitat:** Grassy places. **Flowering Time:** April–September. **Abundance:** Common.

SPRING VETCH (*Vicia lathyroides*) ☐

Height: Low. **Flowers:** Deep lilac, pea shaped, each flower 0.5–0.8 cm long. **Stem:** Prostrate, downy. **Leaves:** Narrow leaflets, 2–4 pairs, unbranched tendrils at ends of leaves. **Habitat:** Sandy ground, especially by the sea. **Flowering time:** April–May. **Abundance:** Locally common.

HOUNDS TONGUE *(Cynoglossum officinale)*

Height: Medium, tall. **Flowers:** Purplish red/maroon, 5 joined petals, each flower up to 1 cm across, heads in clusters. **Stem:** Erect, branched, greyish, downy. **Leaves:** Narrow, downy. **Habitat:** Dry grassy places, dunes. **Flowering Time:** May–August. **Abundance:** Infrequent. **Extra info:** Smells of mice. Fruit with short hooked bristles sticks to fur, clothing etc.

EARLY PURPLE ORCHID *(Orchis mascula)* ☐

Height: Short, medium. **Flowers:** Purple or pink–purple, with a helmet at the top, 3 lobed lip 0.8–1.0 cm wide, smell of tom cats. **Stem:** Erect. **Leaves:** Narrow, oblong, shiny dark green, usually with purple–black lengthwise blotches. **Habitat:** Wood, scrub, grassland, on shingle at Dungeness, which is an unusual habitat. **Flowering Time:** April–June. **Abundance:** Rare.

SELF – HEAL *(Prunella vulgaris)* ☐

Height: Low. **Flowers:** Violet, rarely white or pink, each flower 1.0–1.5 cm long, hooded top,3 lobed lower lip, many flowers together forming an oblong or square head. **Stem:** Square, creeping or erect, downy. **Leaves:** Pointed, oval. **Habitat:** Grassland, bare ground. **Flowering Time:** June–October. **Abundance:** Common. **Extra info:** Believed to have many healing properties.

PURPLE LOOSESTRIFE *(Lythrum salicaria)* ☐

Height: Tall. **Flowers:** Red–purple, 6 petals, each flower 1.0–1.5 cm across. **Stem:** Erect, downy, at least 4 raised lines up stem. **Leaves:** Narrow, lanceolate. **Habitat:** Damp places, especially by rivers. **Flowering Time:** June–August. **Abundance:** Fairly common. **Extra info:** Sap is rich in tannin and has been used for tanning leather.

WATER MINT *(Mentha aquatica)* ☐

Height: Short, medium. **Flowers:** Mauve, lilac or pinkish lilac, 4 petals, each flower 0.7 cm across, many clustered together to form a flower head 2 cm across approx. **Stem:** Square, erect, downy, branched. **Leaves:** Pointed oval, mint scented. **Habitat:** Wet places. **Flowering Time:** July–September. **Abundance:** Occasional. **Extra info:** Leaves were strewn on floors as an air freshener.

BITTERSWEET *(Solanum dulcamara)* ☐

Height: To 2 metres. **Flowers:** Bright purple, 5 joined petals curving backwards, each flower 1.5–2.0 cm across. **Stem:** Scrambling, downy, often grows prostrate at Dungeness. **Leaves:** Pointed oval. **Habitat:** Woods, scrub, hedges, waste places, damp places, shingle. **Flowering Time:** May–September. **Abundance:** Occasional. **Extra info:** Berry poisonous, egg shaped, green, then orange/yellow, red when ripe.

WATER FIGWORT *(Scrophularia auriculata)* ☐

Height: Medium, tall. **Flowers:** Reddish brown, each flower 0.4–1.0 cm across, open mouthed, pouch like. **Stem:** Erect, branched, with raised edges. **Leaves:** Oval, blunt tipped, blunt toothed. **Habitat:** Wet places, pond and stream edges, moist woodland. **Flowering Time:** June–September. **Abundance:** Local.

IVY – LEAVED TOADFLAX *(Cymbalaria muralis)* ☐

Height: Low, creeping. **Flowers:** Lilac or white, yellow spot in centre, each flower 0.8–1.0 cm across, upper lip striped, lower lip in 3 lobes. **Stem:** Trailing, weak. May form mats on shingle. **Leaves:** Palm shaped, like Ivy, lobed. **Habitat:** On walls, waste ground, rocks, shingle beaches. **Flowering Time:** April–October. **Abundance:** Common.

TEASEL *(Dipsacus fullonum)* ☐

Height: Tall. **Flowers:** Pale purple, many small flowers clustered together in a spiny egg shaped cone at top of stem forming a flowerhead 3.0–8.0 cm long. **Stem:** Erect, prickly, branched. **Leaves:** Narrow, prickly, with white pimples. **Habitat:** Bare grassy places, banks of streams, road verges, open woodland. **Flowering Time:** July–August. **Abundance:** Common. **Extra info:** Seeds popular with Goldfinches and flowers popular with butterflies and bees. Dried flower heads still being used to raise nap on cloth.

SPEAR THISTLE *(Cirsium vulgare)* ☐

Height: Medium, tall. **Flowers:** Pink–purple, flowerhead 2.0–4.0 cm across, solitary or loose clustered, bracts under flowerheads have yellow spine tips arching backwards and form a circular shape. **Stem:** Erect, branched, cottony, with sharp spines. **Leaves:** Spiny–tipped, deeply pinnately lobed, prickly hairy above. **Habitat:** Wasteland, roadside, grassland, open woodland. **Flowering Time:** July–October. **Abundance:** Frequent.

LESSER BURDOCK *(Arctium minus)* ☐

Height: Medium, tall. **Flowers:** Purple–red, flowerhead 1.5–3.0 cm wide, bracts below flowerhead with hooked tips. **Stem:** Stout, downy, arching, furrowed. **Leaves:** Oval, heart–shaped, stalks hollow. **Habitat:** Shady, waste places, scrub, hedgebank, roadside, **Flowering Time:** July–September, **Abundance:** Infrequent.

CREEPING THISTLE *(Cirsium arvense)* ☐

Height: Medium, tall. **Flowers:** Lilac or white, flowerhead 1.5–2.5 cm across, like a brush, scented, in clusters. **Stem:** Erect, without prickles, little branched, furrowed. **Leaves:** Prickly, greyish green above, sometimes cottony beneath, wavy and toothed edges, narrow. **Habitat:** Grassy and waste places. **Flowering Time:** June–September. **Abundance:** Common.

Alternative colours: Early Scurvy Grass is included in the white section, but may also be lilac.

SHEEPS BIT SCABIOUS *(Jasione montana)*

Height: Low, short. **Flowers:** Pale blue, each flower 0.5 cm long, many clustered together in a dense rounded flowerhead 1.0–3.0 cm across. **Stem:** Erect or sprawling, downy. **Leaves:** Narrow, may be wavy, bristly. **Habitat:** Dry grassland, sea cliffs, shingle, heaths, dunes. **Flowering Time:** May–September. **Abundance:** Local and infrequent.

EARLY FORGET–ME–NOT *(Myosotis ramosissima)*

Height: Low. **Flowers:** Bright blue, 5 joined petals, each flower 0.2 cm across. **Stem:** Erect or lies on ground and rises at the end, hairy. **Leaves:** Oblong, hairy. **Habitat:** Dry, open places, sandy areas. **Flowering Time:** April–June. **Abundance:** Locally common.

CHANGING FORGET–ME–NOT *(Myosotis discolor)* □

Height: Low, short. **Flowers:** Creamy or pale yellow at first, becoming blue, 5 joined petals, each flower 0.2 cm across, flower stalks curved inwards towards stem and unfold as flowers open. **Stem:** Erect, hairy. **Leaves:** Narrow, hairy. **Habitat:** Bare places, light sandy soils. **Flowering Time:** May–June. **Abundance:** Fairly common.

BUGLE *(Ajuga reptans)* □

Height: Low, short. **Flowers:** Blue, hooded, 3 lobed lower lip with white streaks, each flower 0.5–0.6 cm across. **Stem:** Square, erect, hairy on 2 opposite sides, creeping rooting runners. **Leaves:** Oblong, shiny, in opposite pairs. **Habitat:** Damp woods, grassland. **Flowering Time:** April–June. **Abundance:** Common.
Extra info: Medieval herbalists held this in great esteem as a cure all.

VIPER'S BUGLOSS *(Echium vulgare)*

Height: Short, medium. **Flowers:** Blue, 5 petals, 1.5–2.0 cm long, trumpet shaped, all stamens protruding, buds pinkish red. **Stem:** Erect, bristly, with dark spots. **Leaves:** Hairy, rough, narrow. **Habitat:** Dry open ground, sand dunes, shingle beaches. **Flowering Time:** June–August. **Abundance:** Very common. **Extra info:** Important for moth caterpillars and as a nectar source for bees and other insects.

GERMANDER SPEEDWELL *(Veronica chamaedrys)* ☐

Height: Low, short. **Flowers:** Bright blue, 4 joined petals with white centres, each flower 1.0 cm across. **Stem:** Erect or creeping, 2 opposite lines of hairs on stem. **Leaves:** Pointed oval, toothed edges, hairy. **Habitat:** Grassy places. **Flowering Time:** March–July. **Abundance:** Common.

GROUND IVY *(Glechoma hederacea)* ☐

Height: Low. **Flowers:** Blue violet (rarely pink or white), 1.5–2.2 cm long, flat upper lip, 3 lobed purple spotted lower lip. **Stem:** Creeping, hairy, with long runners which may form a carpet. **Leaves:** Kidney shaped, blunt toothed, long stalked, often reddish purple tinged, aromatic when crushed. **Habitat:** Woods, hedgebanks, grassy and bare areas. **Flowering Time:** March–June. **Abundance:** Very common. **Extra info:** Leaves were the main source of flavouring bitter in beer before the introduction of hops.

BULBOUS BUTTERCUP *(Ranunculus bulbosus)* ☐

Height: Short. **Flowers:** Bright yellow, 5 petals, each flower 1.5–3.0 cm across, flower stalks furrowed, 5 pale yellow sepals below petals turn down. **Stem:** Upright, branched, hairy. **Leaves:** Hairy, 3 lobed, middle lobe stalked. **Habitat:** Dry grassland, preferably on lime. **Flowering Time:** May–June. **Abundance:** Uncommon.

AUTUMN HAWKBIT *(Leontodon autumnalis)* ☐

Height: Low, short. **Flowers:** Golden yellow, shaped like a dandelion, flowerhead 1.0–3.5 cm across, outer florets often streaked reddish beneath. **Stem:** Erect, branched 2 or 3 times, hairless or very few hairs. **Leaves:** Shiny, deeply lobed, pointed end to leaf. **Habitat:** Meadows, grassland, road verges. **Flowering Time:** June–October. **Abundance:** Very common.

YELLOW HORNED POPPY *(Glaucium flavum)* ☐

Height: Medium, tall. **Flowers:** Yellow, 4 petals, each flower 6–9 cm across, each one only lasts one day. **Stem:** Branching, greyish green. **Leaves:** Wavy edged, waxy, pinnately lobed, with hairs. **Habitat:** Shingle, sandy beaches, disturbed areas, bare and waste places inland. **Flowering Time:** June–September. **Abundance:** Very common. **Extra info:** Seed pods up to 30 cm long, sickle shaped. Plant has unpleasant smell.

WELD *(Reseda luteola)*

Height: Tall. **Flowers:** Greenish yellow, 4 petals, each flower 0.4–0.5 cm across, flowers in a long, narrow spike. **Stem:** Erect, not branched, stiff. **Leaves:** Long, narrow, wavy edged. **Habitat:** Disturbed ground. **Flowering Time:** June–September. **Abundance:** Very common. **Extra info:** Cultivated in Kent until recently for a yellow dye.

BITING STONECROP *(Sedum acre)*

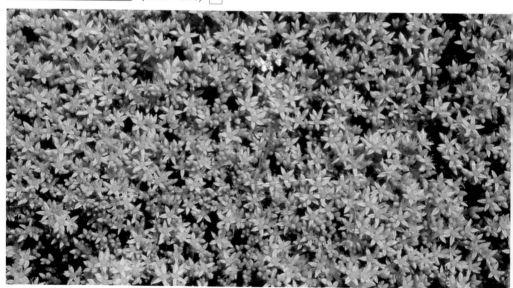

Height: Low. **Flowers:** Bright yellow, 5 petals, each flower 1.2 cm across. **Stem:** Creeping, smooth, fleshy, forms a mat. **Leaves:** Cylindrical, fleshy, taste peppery, (hence English name). **Habitat:** Dry, bare places. **Flowering Time:** May–July. **Abundance:** Common. **Extra info:** Also known as Wall Pepper.

AGRIMONY *(Agrimonia eupatoria)* ☐

Height: Medium. **Flowers:** Yellow, 5 petals, each flower 0.5–0.8 cm across, in a spike, apricot scented. **Stem:** Erect, hairy, often reddish. **Leaves:** Pinnate, toothed. **Habitat:** Dry grassy places. **Flowering Time:** June–August. **Abundance:** Fairly common.

CREEPING CINQUEFOIL *(Potentilla reptans)* ☐

Height: Low, short. **Flowers:** Yellow, 5 petals, flowerhead 1.7–2.5 cm across, flowers solitary on long stalks. **Stem:** Creeping and rooting, up to 1 metre long, often reddish. **Leaves:** 5–7 toothed leaflets. **Habitat:** Hedgebank, grassland, wasteground. **Flowering Time:** June–September. **Abundance:** Common.

SILVERWEED *(Potentilla anserina)*

Height: Low, short. **Flowers:** Yellow, 5 petals, each flower 1.5–2.0 cm across. **Stem:** Hairy, creeping. **Leaves:** Pinnate toothed, silvery silky, especially underneath. **Habitat:** Damp, grassy places. **Flowering Time:** May–August. **Abundance:** Fairly common.

GORSE *(Ulex europaeus)*

Height: Tall shrub to 2.5 metres. **Flowers:** Golden yellow, pea–shaped, 2 cm across, coconut scented. **Stem:** Branched, spiny, rigid. **Leaves:** Appear as evergreen, rigid, furrowed spines. **Habitat:** Heathland, grassland. **Flowering Time:** All year round. **Abundance:** Very common.

BROOM *(Cytisus scoparius)* ☐

Height: Tall shrub, lower or prostrate on shingle by sea. **Flowers:** Yellow, pea shaped, each flower 1.6–1.8 cm across. **Stem:** Spineless, ridged, branched, erect. **Leaves:** Narrow in leaflets of 3s. **Habitat:** Grassland, heathland, open woodland, sea shingle. **Flowering Time:** April–June. **Abundance:** Very common.

MEADOW VETCHLING *(Lathyrus pratensis)* ☐

Height: Short, medium, tall. **Flowers:** Yellow, pea shaped, each flower 1.5–1.8 cm across, 4–12 flowers together. **Stem:** Scrambling, angled. **Leaves:** Pairs of narrow grey green leaflets with tendrils. **Habitat:** Grassy places. **Flowering Time:** May–August. **Abundance:** Common.

RIBBED MELILOT *(Melilotus officinalis)*

Height: Medium, tall. **Flowers:** Yellow, pea shaped, each flower 0.5–0.6 cm long with a short stalk, all on a long spike. **Stem:** Erect, branched. **Leaves:** Narrow, toothed leaflets in 3s. **Habitat:** Bare and waste ground. **Flowering Time:** June–September. **Abundance:** Occasional. **Extra info:** Pods hairless, brown when ripe and wrinkled with ridges going across which distinguishes from similar **Tall Melilot**, *(Melilotus altissima)*, which has hairy black ripe pods with net veins across.

BIRDS FOOT TREFOIL *(Lotus corniculatus)*

Height: Low, creeping. **Flowers:** Yellow, often tinged orange or red, pea shaped, each flower 1.0–1.6 cm long, 2–8 flowers in a head. **Stem:** Almost hairless, rarely with hairs. **Leaves:** Five oval leaflets. **Habitat:** Grassy places. **Flowering Time:** May–September. **Abundance:** Fairly common. **Extra info:** Also known as Eggs and Bacon because of flower colour. Seed pods shaped like a bird's foot. Important food plant for Common Blue Butterfly caterpillars.

BLACK MEDICK *(Medicago lupulina)* □

Photo by H. Silk

Height: Low. **Flowers:** Bright yellow, pea–shaped, 10–50 clustered together in a head 0.3–0.8 cm across. **Stem:** Prostrate, sprawling or becoming erect, downy. **Leaves:** 3 broad leaflets together, downy, toothed, each one with a very small point. **Habitat:** Bare and grassy places. **Flowering Time:** April–October. **Abundance:** Fairly common. **Extra info:** Curved seed heads black when ripe.

LARGE–FLOWERED EVENING PRIMROSE *(Oenothera glazoviana)* □

Height: Medium, tall. **Flowers:** Pale yellow, 4 petals, each flower 8.0–10 cm across. **Stem:** Erect, hairy, red spotted, leafy. **Leaves:** Narrow, toothed, crinkly margins. **Habitat:** Bare and waste places, dunes. **Flowering Time:** June–September, **Abundance:** Common. **Extra info:** Flowers can be watched as they open in the evening.

WILD PARSNIP *(Pastinaca sativa)* ☐

Height: Medium, tall. **Flowers:** Yellow, each flower 1.5 mm across, forming clusters 5–15 cm across. **Stem:** Erect, branched, hairy, hollow, furrowed. **Leaves:** Pinnate, toothed, rough. **Habitat:** Grassy and bare places. **Flowering Time:** June–September. **Abundance:** Very common. **Extra info:** Leaves smell of parsnip. Garden variety developed from this wild plant.

LADY'S BEDSTRAW *(Galium verum)* ☐

Height: Low, short. **Flowers:** Bright yellow, 4 petals, each flower 0.2–0.3 cm across. **Stem:** Square, creeping at the base, almost upright when in flower. **Leaves:** Very narrow, linear in whorls of 8–12, dark green, shiny, margins rolled back. **Habitat:** Dry grassy places. **Flowering Time:** June–September. **Abundance:** Variable. **Extra info:** Formerly used dried in mattresses to give sweet, fragrant smell. "Lady's" from idea that Virgin Mary laid on it to give birth to Jesus. Flowers were used as a rennet substitute for curdling milk.

ROCK SAMPHIRE *(Crithmum maritimum)*

Height: Short, medium. **Flowers:** Pale yellow green, each flower up to 0.2 cm across, many clustered in flowerheads 3–6 cm across. **Stem:** Solid, ridged, spreading. **Leaves:** Needle like, fleshy, greyish. **Habitat:** Cliffs, rocks, sand, shingle. **Flowering Time:** July–September. **Abundance:** Local.

FRINGED WATER–LILY *(Nymphoides peltata)* ☐

Height: Low, floating in water. **Flowers:** Yellow, 5 fringed petals, each flower 3.0 cm across. **Stem:** Floating. **Leaves:** Floating, rounded, kidney shaped, purple underneath. **Habitat:** Still and slow moving fresh water. **Flowering Time:** June–September. **Abundance:** Local. **Extra info:** May form yellow masses in water.

GREAT MULLEIN *(Verbascum thapsus)* ☐

Height: Tall. **Flowers:** Bright yellow, 5 petals, each flower 1.5–2.5 cm across, lots together in a dense spike. **Stem:** Erect, round, white, with a thick woolly down, usually unbranched. **Leaves:** Stem leaves broad lanceo-late, whitish woolly, downy. **Habitat:** Dry grassy, bare places. **Flowering Time:** June–August. **Abundance:** Fairly common. **Extra info:** Fluffy hairs were scraped off the leaves and used as candlewicks.

COMMON TOADFLAX *(Linaria vulgaris)* ☐

Height: Short, medium. **Flowers:** Yellow with orange on lower lip, pouch shaped, flower-head 1.5–2.5 cm in length with a long spur, heads on a spike. **Stem:** Erect. **Leaves:** Narrow, grey green. **Habitat:** Grassland, wasteground, hedgebank, bare places. **Flowering Time:** July–August. **Abundance:** Fairly common.

HONEYSUCKLE *(Lonicera periclymenum)* ☐

Height: To 6 metres, climbing. **Flowers:** Creamy, often reddish outside, orange after pollination, 2 lipped, trumpet shaped, very fragrant, especially at night. **Stem:** Woody, twists clockwise. **Leaves:** Oval, not toothed, pointed. **Habitat:** Woodland, hedgebank, scrub, rocks. **Flowering Time:** June–September. **Abundance:** Fairly common. **Extra info:** Red poisonous berry.

PINEAPPLE MAYWEED *(Matricaria discoidea)* ☐

Height: Low, short. **Flowers:** Greenish yellow, cone shaped, 0.5–0.8 cm across. **Stem:** Erect, branched. **Leaves:** Threadlike, narrow branching segments, 2–3 pinnate. **Habitat:** Waste places, tracks, paths, well trodden places. **Flowering Time:** May–November. **Abundance:** Common. **Extra info:** Smells strongly of pineapple when crushed.

JERSEY CUDWEED *(Gnaphalium luteoalbum)* ☐

Height: Short, medium. **Flowers:** Pale yellow, each flower 0.4–0.5 cm across, egg shaped, clustered together on stem, heads with red stigmas. **Stem:** Erect, little branched, with woolly hairs. **Leaves:** Narrow, greyish, woolly. **Habitat:** Sandy heaths, dunes. **Flowering Time:** June–August. **Abundance:** Rare. **Extra info:** Colonised Dungeness in 1996 in bare sandy areas near gravel pit margins. May be seen at RSPB Dungeness.

COMMON FLEABANE *(Pulicaria dysenterica)* ☐

Height: Medium. **Flowers:** Golden yellow, flowerhead 1.5–3.0 cm across, like a daisy, central disc florets and outer ray florets golden yellow. **Stem:** Erect, softly hairy, branched. **Leaves:** Narrow, wavy edged, downy. **Habitat:** Damp, grassy places. **Flowering Time:** July–August. **Abundance:** Frequent. **Extra info:** Very popular with butterflies. Was used as an insecticide; first part of the scientific name means flea and the second part refers to its use for dysentery in ancient times.

COMMON RAGWORT *(Senecio jacobaea)* ☐

Height: Medium, tall. **Flowers:** Yellow, flowerhead 1.5–2.5 cm across, with central disc florets and outer ray florets, heads in dense flat topped clusters, inner bracts under flowerheads with black tips. **Stem:** Erect, branched, ridged. **Leaves:** Pinnate, lobed with blunt ends, rather cottony underneath. **Habitat:** Dry grassy places. **Flowering Time:** June–November. **Abundance:** Very common. **Extra info:** An important food plant for the black and yellow striped cinnabar moth caterpillar and an important source of nectar for late flying butterflies. When dried with hay, large quantities cause liver damage to cattle and horses over a period of time, but sheep are not affected. **Oxford Ragwort** *Senecio squalidus* (not shown) has pointed ends to the lobed leaves and all the bracts under the flowerhead have black tips.

46

STICKY GROUNDSEL *(Senecio viscosus)* ☐

Height: Short, medium. **Flowers:** Pale yellow, each flowerhead 0.6–1.0 cm across. **Stem:** Erect, branched, very sticky, hairy. **Leaves:** Pinnate, lobed, dark green, very sticky. **Habitat:** Bare and waste places. **Flowering:** July–September. **Abundance:** Fairly common. **Extra info:** Unpleasant smelling plant.

CARLINE THISTLE *(Carlina vulgaris)* ☐

Height: Low, short. **Flowers:** Yellow brown centre, outer disc florets light brownish yellow, flowerhead 3.0–4.0 cm across. **Stem:** Erect, spiny, often purplish. **Leaves:** Lobed, pinnate, prickly. **Habitat:** Grassland, dunes, on lime. **Flowering Time:** July–September. **Abundance:** Fairly common. **Extra info:** Popular with bees.

PERENNIAL SOWTHISTLE *(Sonchus arvensis)* ☐

Height: Tall. **Flowers:** Rich yellow, shaped like a dandelion, flowerhead 4–5 cm across, heads in clusters. Bracts under flowerhead with sticky yellow glands. **Stem:** Erect, branching. **Leaves:** Pinnate, lobed, soft spines on edges, shiny green above, greyish beneath, clasping stem with rounded lobes. **Habitat:** Bare and waste ground. **Flowering Time:** July–October. **Abundance:** Fairly common.

COMMON CATS EAR *(Hypochaeris radicata)* ☐

Height: Short, medium. **Flowers:** Yellow, shaped like a dandelion, flowerhead 2–4 cm across, solitary. **Stem:** Erect, little branched, no leaves, with scale like bracts, like little ears. **Leaves:** Narrow, indented, roughly hairy, blunt or rounded end to leaf. **Habitat:** Dry, grassy places. **Flowering Time:** June–September. **Abundance:** Local.

BRISTLY OX–TONGUE *(Picris echioides)*

Height: Medium. **Flowers:** Pale yellow, flowerhead 2.0–2.5 cm across, heads in a cluster. **Stem:** Erect, branched, bristly, furrowed. **Leaves:** Narrow, wavy edged, bristly, with many whitish pimples. **Habitat:** Rough, grassy places. **Flowering Time:** June–November. **Abundance:** Fairly common.

MOUSE EAR HAWKWEED *(Pilosella officinarum)* ☐

Height: Low, short. **Flowers:** Lemon yellow, shaped like a dandelion, flowerhead 2–3 cm across, solitary, outer florets often reddish beneath. **Stem:** Erect, unbranched, leafless, hairy. **Leaves:** Linear to oblong, untoothed, stiff white hairs above and below, also white soft felted hairs below. **Habitat:** Bare and grassy places. **Flowering Time:** May–October. **Abundance:** Common.

YELLOW IRIS *(Iris pseudacorus)* ☐

Height: Tall. **Flowers:** Bright yellow, 6 petals, narrow at the base, often purple veined, each flower 8–10 cm across, 1–3 flowers together. **Stem:** Erect, branched. **Leaves:** Narrow, sword shaped. **Habitat:** Marshes, by or in fresh water. **Flowering Time:** June–August. **Abundance:** Common. **Extra info:** Also known as Yellow Flag.

Alternative Colours: Nottingham Catchfly is included in the white section, but may also be a creamy colour. Wood Sage is included in the white section, but may also be greenish yellow.

EARLY SCURVY – GRASS *(Cochlearia danica)* ☐

Height: Low, short. **Flowers:** White or lilac, 4 petals, each flower 0.4–0.5 cm across. **Stem:** Branched, upright. **Leaves:** Fleshy, stalked, lower stem leaves ivy shaped. **Habitat:** Sandy and stony places, especially by the sea. Now spreading inland on road verges and central reservations with winter road salting. **Flowering Time:** January–September. **Abundance:** Fairly common. **Extra info:** Contains a high Vitamin C content and was used in the treatment of scurvy.

HEDGE BINDWEED *(Calystegia sepium)* ☐

Height: Tall. **Flowers:** White, open trumpet shaped, each flower 3–4 cm across. **Stem:** Creeping or climbing anticlockwise. **Leaves:** Arrow shaped. **Habitat:** Hedges, wasteland, woods. **Flowering Time:** June–September. **Abundance:** Widespread.

Height: Medium. **Flowers:** White, 4 petals, each flower 1.0–1.5 cm across, flowers clustered in flattish topped branching heads. **Stem:** Erect, branching below, smooth. **Leaves:** Waxy grey, very fleshy, crinkly lobes or teeth, wavy margins. New leaves in spring purplish. **Habitat:** Seashore, on sand and shingle. **Flowering Time:** June–August. **Abundance:** Very common. **Extra info:** Grows in clumps. Long tap root keeps it stable in shingle and enables it to obtain water from as deep as 6 metres. Round corky fruiting heads float on sea water and assist in its dispersal.

SHEPHERD'S CRESS (*Teesdalia nudicaulis*)

Height: Low, short. **Flowers:** White, 4 unequal petals, each flower 0.2 cm across. **Stem:** Erect, almost hairless and almost leafless. **Leaves:** Lobed in a ground hugging rosette. **Habitat:** Sandy and gravelly places. **Flowering Time:** April–June. **Abundance:** Fairly common. **Extra info:** Seed pod oval, blunt or notched. In Kent, restricted to Dungeness and Hythe areas.

BLACKTHORN (*Prunus spinosa*)

Height: Tall, thicket forming shrub, 1–4 metres, (low, short, almost prostrate at Dungeness). **Flowers:** White, 5 petals, each flower 1.0–1.5 cm across, flowers appear before leaves. **Stem:** Branched, thorny, rigid. **Leaves:** Oval, toothed, not shiny. **Habitat:** Scrub, hedges, woodland, (shingle at Dungeness). **Flowering Time:** March–May. **Abundance:** Very common. **Extra info:** Blue–black very sour fruit is the sloe, used in sloe gin.

54

DUSTY MILLER *(Cerastium tomentosum)* ☐

Height: Low, short. **Flowers:** White, 5 deeply notched petals, each flower 1.5–2.5 cm across. **Stem:** Branched, erect or sprawling, densely matted, soft, hairy. **Leaves:** Narrow, margins rolled under, silvery all over with white hairs, soft. **Habitat:** Dry, sunny places. **Flowering Time:** May–July. **Abundance:** Local. **Extra info:** Garden escapee. Also known as Snow–in–Summer.

SEA CAMPION *(Silene uniflora)* ☐

Height: Short. **Flowers:** White, 5 deeply forked petals, each flower 2.0–2.5 cm across; below this is a bladder like cylindrical inflated calyx with red veining. **Stem:** Erect flowering stem with cushions of non flowering prostrate shoots. **Leaves:** Narrow, waxy, slightly bluish. **Habitat:** Shingle, cliffs, coast, mountains inland. **Flowering Time:** June–August. **Abundance:** Very common.

NOTTINGHAM CATCHFLY *(Silene nutans)* ☐

Height: Medium. **Flowers:** Creamy white or pale pink, 5 rolled back deeply forked petals, drooping flower 1.8 cm across, fragrant, closed in daytime and open at night. **Stem:** Erect, upper part sticky. **Leaves:** Upper leaves narrow, pointed, all hairy. **Habitat:** Shingle beaches, dry areas, limestone cliffs. **Flowering Time:** May–August. **Abundance:** Locally abundant in this area, but rare in Kent. **Extra info:** Important food plant for many moth caterpillars.

WHITE CAMPION *(Silene latifolia)* ☐

Height: Medium, tall. **Flowers:** White, 5 deeply forked petals, each flower 2.5–3.0 cm across. **Stem:** Erect, branching, sticky, hairy. **Leaves:** Narrow, hairy, pointed. **Habitat:** Wasteland, hedge banks, arable ground, road verges. **Flowering Time:** May–October. **Abundance:** Infrequent.

ENGLISH STONECROP *(Sedum anglicum)* ☐

Height: Low. **Flowers:** White, pink beneath, 5 petals, each flower 1.2 cm across. **Stem:** Branched, forming a mat. **Leaves:** Fleshy, cylindrical, waxy grey, usually red tinged. **Habitat:** Coastal shingle, dry grassland, acid rocks. **Flowering Time**: June–September. **Abundance:** Locally common.

WILD CARROT *(Daucus carota)* ☐

Height: Medium. **Flowers:** White, each flower 0.2–0.3 cm across with many clustered together to form a flattish head 3–7 cm across, central flower often dark red. Green bracts hang down beneath the flowerhead. **Stem:** Erect, branched, ridged, hairy. **Leaves:** Finely divided, feathery, pinnate. **Habitat:** Near the sea, grassy places, roadside, hedgebank. **Flowering Time:** June–September. **Abundance:** Common. **Extra info:** Fruiting head closes up and resembles a bird's nest. Caterpillars of the Sussex Emerald moth, found only at Dungeness in Britain, use Wild Carrot as their food plant.

HEATH BEDSTRAW *(Galium saxatile)* ☐

Height: Low, short. **Flowers:** White, 4 petals, each flower 0.3 cm across, many clustered together, scented. **Stem:** Square, smooth, may be prostrate, branched. **Leaves:** Very narrow, in whorls of 6–8. **Habitat:** Dry grassy, heathy places. **Flowering Time:** June–August. **Abundance:** Fairly common.

SCENTLESS MAYWEED *(Tripleurospermum inodorum)* ☐

Height: Short, medium. **Flowers:** White spreading outer ray florets, yellow solid dome shaped centre of disc florets, almost scentless, flowerhead 1.5–4.5 cm across. **Stem:** Erect or sprawling, branched. **Leaves:** Threadlike, feathery, pinnate. **Habitat:** Bare or disturbed ground. **Flowering Time:** April–November. **Abundance:** Common.

59

WOOD SAGE *(Teucrium scorodonia)* ☐

Height: Short, medium. **Flowers:** Greenish yellow to white, maroon stamens protruding over 0.5–0.9 cm long lip, honey scented. **Stem:** Square, erect, branched, hairy. **Leaves:** Heart shaped, toothed, wrinkled. **Habitat:** Grassland, heaths,dunes. **Flowering Time:** July–September. **Abundance:** Very common. **Extra info:** Important for insects, especially bumble bees, because it has lots of nectar. Dodder (pg 17) often scrambling over it.

SCENTED MAYWEED (Matricaria recutita) ☐

Height: Short, medium. **Flowers:** White outer ray florets which turn down soon after flowers open, yellow hollow centre of disc florets, flowerhead 1.2–2.2 cm across, scented. **Stem:** Erect, branched. **Leaves:** Threadlike, feathery, pinnate. **Habitat:** Waste ground, arable fields on sandy soil. **Flowering Time:** May–July. **Abundance:** Infrequent.

YARROW (Achillea millefolium) ☐

Height: Short, medium. **Flowers:** White or pink, each flower 0.4–0.6 cm across, 5 outer ray florets with creamy central disc florets in dense flower heads, scented. **Stem:** Erect, furrowed, downy, branched. **Leaves:** Feathery, narrow pinnate, dark green. **Habitat:** Grassy places. **Flowering Time:** June–November. **Abundance:** Infrequent.

Alternative Colours: Soapwort, Dog Rose, Bramble, Common Storksbill, Musk Mallow, Foxglove, Red Valerian are included in the pink, red, scarlet, section but may also be white or whitish.
Viper's Bugloss is included in the blue section, but may also be white or whitish.

61

Photographic Explanation.

Photographing the flowers was a challenging labour of love. Dungeness poses two main problems – ever present wind and intense light levels. Even with the lightest breeze, this presents as a gale using a close-up lens on an individual flower/seed head.

The immense amount of light from large skies intensified by reflection from shingle often bleaches out the colour of lighter hued flowers and the UV alters the colour of blues – e.g. Viper's Bugloss. Photos, where possible were taken either morning or afternoon to get more detail.

An added problem for me, was that, living 20 miles inland, suitable weather for photos at home did not always translate to the same at Dungeness which often has its own weather pattern.

    Barbara Gray.

English Index.

Scientific Index.